U U O U

U U O U

M.G. Martin

For Tess Patalano

Touching Exhibition

but waking next to you is like bathing in honey, only to realize that instead of oxygen, the air is composed of infinite tongues. i'm saying you do heavy things to me. & how you hum in the morning. your buzz thickening until the whole of the room is contained in the sound of your you. the sound of you breaking the horizon is so loud it turns red & breaks people's ears. in this way, i'm saying you are like a sunrise that prevails over sound. & when i see you standing next to fire i become jealous of the way the heat touches you. lapping over you without effort or the burden of self. i want to make a grand gesture, so i say, *we are here but somewhere a fire starts itself*. i'm saying the fire always wins. & when our house is on fire & the storm is electric, i will dig a hole for you to lie in while i stand in the rain, head tilted back, mouth & eyes agape. i'm saying i will grow larger as the branches of electricity travel toward the earth. with arms outstretched i'm saying i will not let you get electrocuted.

length

i use the sky as an instrument to practice seeing the calm, calm as the clothes that hide me. we drink coffee. someone is driving a jeep deep into egypt, and there are millions of fireworks that wash the moon with color. i can see the rains gather, before the blue speaks of desire and flushes grey, before we are in charge of eating, and even before the winter goes mad on account of a frozen swarm of bumblebees. your length. i wash myself with your length. we live where love is measured by the length it must travel until it inhabits the entirety of your you. therefore, we drink coffee and rename love, length. therefore, i am naked and washing myself with your length. your length is a cosmic tone of mental therapy. i'm sicker by the day and buying high-powered telescopes. i need to practice seeing. only the skies can shout, "hey, look at me! i'm the best!" my bad, i always confuse can with should. always the brain is a type of vacuum.

exhalation mausoleum

i am building a portable mausoleum to mourn every one of your exhalations. i will carry it on my back & follow you to every place. when you stop at every place i will use the telescope i have built to look inside of you. the telescope is able to look into the insides of your ovaries, to the place where your breath comes from. before i use the telescope, i will collect your exhalations at every place. at every place children will ask what is in the mausoleum strapped to my back. i will let the children climb inside of the mausoleum. getting out, they will say it is dark & empty inside, but that it smells like the place they were born from. the children will ask me what that even means at every place. i am building an abstract language out of your exhalations. the language is called something. the language does look like children tho & it is spoken at every place. you have been to all of them & behind you is a man with a mausoleum strapped to his back at every place.

we found a kind of love called time travel

we met in the middle of a wealthy disaster.
we were playing tender buttons.
we were rotating the crime, we were parking
the bullet & expanding with our mouths.

we only touched in the diagonal.
we found a kind of love called time travel.
or maybe it was called life in nudity
with the possibility of you.

we upgraded the future by committing crimes
against divorce. we sexed the flowers tense
coagulated the butter, we holy thieves.
we sunk in. we were behind the telephone
waiting. we committed crimes in the elevator
using only our tongues. we made backbones
anything but mundane. we found it
everywhere. we inverted ourselves
with the water running beneath the strange sink.

what horse hooves turn into after the horse is over

what adheres me to you is not that you are glue, but that
you are the idea of sticking to something. the possibility
that i will one day become tinfoil & stick to you while
holding all of your you inside of me. holding as
adherence, as the idea of glue. if i were your blood, i'd
encourage you to cut your finger, so that after i dried, i
could look at the world while holding your skin
together. it says sticky. you are a state of magic, like the
way your blood swims through your body while you
are still as & in sleep. like the way you shoot through a
subway tunnel by sitting, still as a tattoo that can't make
shadows. the wind is invisible. the wind is invisible
blood. the wind is invisible.

arachis hypogaea

i open the refrigerator and there it is. the peanut butter
staring me in the face, telling me that my face will move
in on itself as it ages. & the next thing i know i don't.
all peanuts aside, new ways of sound are invented when
you stand anywhere. you are vibrant & i'm into sound.
here i am, sound. here is my face, peanut butter. when i
feel too many things at once, i take refuge in my place
of repose. i sit like the shadow of a peanut flower in my
place of repose. my place is a thought, is *the* thought:
that together we will wait to expire together. my love,
did you know the stalk of the peanut flower bends itself
toward the ground? & that after self-pollination, the
peanut flower buries its own ovary in the soil? my love
isn't that how poetry works? my love can we just wait,
or must we pretend to do things until our date of
expiration? either way, i will always be within arm's
length of your veins: as the flowers fade, as the flowers
wither.

fortified legs

in one week we will have not talked for one week. this makes my furniture sag, frowning at the corners of their various furniture mouths. i've been baking a cake for you for two years & it will be finished in one week. i will have to take pictures of it, sing to it & blow out its candles while you are in another kitchen eating something not called cake. i like to think that we are each a leg connected to the same body, a somebody of small importance, someone of mediocrity, connected to the ground by two vitamin d fortified legs. but what to do with this cake? i might wear it as a helmet. perhaps, i can put a leash on it & name it 'pet rock,' walking it from one side of the kitchen table to the other. most likely, i will lie in bed, cuddling the cake, staring at the sloppy cursive. the sloppy cursive of frosted gel that says, 'i'm trying.' i like to think about living in a furniture store, where the leather doesn't smell like you & where i'm reminded of children eating a cheap, supermarket birthday cake, not knowing any better, about anything.

i am collecting your hair from this shower drain to put into a jar. i am growing you inside of a jar like a sea monkey. i am composting a you stew. it may be too much to ask. expecting to find every bellybutton lint, fingernail & drain hair that has fallen off of you. this is called chemistry of the heart. this is why i am licking the corners of your cereal bowl, looking for you. your artifacts are my sasquatch, my loch ness monster, my sea monkey. yes, reality has been suspended for the rest of the year & the one after that & all the way until reality becomes a lack thereof. this is called chemistry of the heart. there is a reason i am obsessed with the size of the whole pierced into your ear. but i don't know what it is. it is what i am growing inside of a jar: a you stew.

eat me like fruit flesh

you began forcing yourself into my general being the moment i began looking at you. this was the first tangible moment of fruit trees. five years ago i would have said you are the reason pomegranates are poems. five years later i count your elbows, over & over. the way you step out of the shower is a variation on a theme called eat me like fruit flesh. my body is filled with empty trash bags. at the beach all of the sand moves toward your fingers. i think they are magnets.

because these things happen, there is a piece of glass in your foot. it's wet you say. i offer my teeth to your foot and say: it looks like red syrup coming out hot. the line in your foot is now open, a gash of thick wet red heat. a balloon really is nothing without the color of blood you say. this is the point of two smile touches. wouldn't it be swell if the stars turned red & drew wet lines toward each other's heat says the radio voice. maybe, probably not we say. i put a band-aid on your foot with my teeth & say: where is the line at which we evolve into wet heat? i'm trying to find that line, it is where i will leave all of my me stuff. i will come back & place my eyeballs in your sockets. then, you will find that line & place your you stuff next to mine, in a pile of thick wet red hot we stuff.

6,000 miles apart, which is more in kilometers

i'm missing you like as though you lived on the side of a milk carton. i'm dreaming about singing, "if i was your girlfriend," a wtf? written by prince, to you, while we, ride camels, through the fat middle of a k-mart in iowa. i'm in this dream that probably happens because grandmothers always die, even mine. i'm copping out again because i don't have enough money for a ring but eventually i will make you one of those tin foil numbers. i'm having heart palpitations & the size of my heart is that of a watermelon & if i'm lucky: you will eat my seeds until i am not a giant in this world where you live & i am not real. i'm not the shit, but you're mine: in the non-fecal, romantic way. i'm making a commitment to do many illegal things for you & your love, just in case you pick my number. i'm trying to try hard enough to try harder, but i'm pining for you like a douglas fir in a plastic christmas tree factory. so just hold on just a minute & fall in love with me, you: you, o you.

for serious

i walked across things
to where you were
to show you that i could
chaos my face
with your irises until
we became a song
about the tenderness
of water falling onto plastic
and the sound it makes

i walked across things
to where you were
and turned off every river

i walked across things
to where you were
to where the geometry
of your feet was narcotic
to where your ears bloomed
with real life creeping
bougainvillea
which i tied around
my authentic wrists
before i offered the oblivion
of my open mouth to you

no wonder we are mostly water

the river is safe to drink
unless it is made
of lightning or loss

but if the river is made
of loss then i'm sorry
but you have to drink
from it

that river
we continue to circle back to
that river that continues to laugh
at us and our book length loss

the river is never impressed
with itself or that our vision
continues to decline on account
of an inability to climb
outside of ourselves   just kidding

it is sad that my sister is a legitimate ghost
the only effort i can make is to become
a place that is always on fire
somewhere something someplace
always on fire

when you see that river
hold on to yourself   just kidding
you're alive and that's abstract enough

what a time to be alive with a mouth
full of canary feathers

river
get out of my zone of catastrophe
i don't need any
help double crossing myself
i'm doing just fine
as a human maybe

we poison the water to erase the river
loss   just kidding

that lightning though
that's what's up isn't it

wet eraser

my deer face

the days become desperate
the trees grow lungs
& breathe their own air
to empty themselves of song

they are desperate for the time
before animal when earth
was only full of air

basically i love you difficult
like trying to kill
a velociraptor in the snow
like owning a piece of sky & pulling
thunder from the trunk of your body

far out in the ocean is a boat
with an anchor too short to succeed

you are the warm heat on the face of child

far out in the future is a dying me
with only one regret to have lived like smoke
inside of your closed fist
inside of a glass shoe filled with sunlight
inside of the other side of sunlight

the inside parts of my veins are the temperature
& color of anticipation of exploded deer

i am thinking tree & searching for your mouth
i am thinking snow & bleeding your sap

there is no complex solution
to remove splinters from your lungs
open your chest with me touch the inside

use this rope to attach the face
of a deer to the face
of my face use this rope to climb
all over me like i am cliff in ruins

i am dumb with snow

i'm trying to be close
to you
until i can't. until i can
extinguish sunlight.

i am naked on a mountain
i have two fists & am
my own birthstone.

i am caught between sound
& the ear.

i am dumb with snow
falling on the mountain.
it is so big the mountain

is so big & i am trying
to measure
my perceptions

with a blank palette
of invisible imaginary
made up colors.

there is a sadness in english.
the mountain rubs

up on the sky & the sky
becomes colder

the closer you come

to the sun

unmeltable

wherever the snow refuses
the sun is where we meet
for the millionth time   all million everything
i'm obsessed with your dead skin and formulating a
plan
to learn to touch things
whether it's haunt or hunt i will do that to you

here we are   again   swallowing all the city's snow
as though the universe will only end
when it's run out of things to steal and reproduce as
something new
so we're good

who does sadness turn to
when the moon finally explodes
after all these decades we are starting to smell
like all these decades

so   yes i'm selling off my own agency
to become the target of your tongue
and its language to become endless
to open my body in the middle
of july and find that my body
is filled with snow
so   yes i am gifting you
my body's snow

Waterfalls Are Lazy

waterfalls are lazy but incredibly beautiful

help! i am still alive and the rain is ugly which means
i'm wrong

i want to commit suicide by eating black diamonds &
be perfect like my sister

soon the oceans won't exist & the world will be a
canyon full of what we can't imagine

drugs are the answer as fire is the answer as peace is the
answer as water is unable to death

it is not enough to haunt graffiti you must abandon
your house & sleep with your skin out

waterfalls are lazy but incredibly beautiful

the danger is not in the reflection or the mirror but in
the eyes

become the hand that is the cloth that covers my body

to harness your being is to fool yourself into being but
i collect human teeth

as the house slides off the edge of a cliff you are just
waking up in the house, goodbye

what if what if were just what if & not the palette of

fear

omg guess what i love you you are literally everything
since the big bang & you glow in the dark

fill yourself with emptiness keep eyes open until it is
time

postcard

placing my organs into your absence is a way of filling
your absence

filling my organs with passion fruit
finding proof of extraterrestrial life

the absence of your you   an   hourglass
filled with sulfur

what's the rent like behind your lids
i'm trying to get   there

baby grand pianos cascading over waterfall cliffs
waterfalls and the promise of bread

bread made of promises
the promise of an us

we walk and scream in technicolor
either i need two hundred dollars or to exist
as a streak of rainbow sherbet

we are learning to yield fruit   almost there
we have the same number of bones
spray paint was invented to adorn our organs

it is inside of the choices that govern the way we carry
an umbrella in the sunlight. it is inside the moment the
battery spends its last drop of juice on artificial light. it
is inside the organ played by our future ghost. it is
inside the place our discarded potential goes to
procrastinate. it is inside it can't be because it can & is.
it is inside of the slipping between our fingers. it is
inside of the violence of the last light of moon hitting
an ocean floor. it is inside the sleep turning you into a
temporary statue of liquidity. it is inside the return of
a sorrow only known on an ocean floor. it is inside
you when you are inside an ocean & the moon is
glowing electric black.

a lone piece of electrical wire

i am using time to move
through my life. many hours
per inch. two days per step.
& what dawn is this? shaping
whether i am here or missing.
shaping though i try to be more
than one color. in the morning
the feet are useless. & still
i am alone a lone piece
of electric wire. i have
no name for time
to usurp. i become fat
with worry i laugh
at fire. i am a fool.
i spend a half year
opening my eyes & still cannot
find food. one arm in a slice of sun
light, the rest of the body
saying leave me be. i am living
backwards & upside down. i am
never smoking & always of smoke.
lungs of gold i am the color
of mourning of sounds that continue
after the ears falls off.
each step the delay
in the echo.
rain
i am unzipping my psyche.
wind

an entire human elevator.
light
one foot at a time without time.
rain
i am finished before i am finished.
wind
i am the fire started to save
myself from
light

milk fire

the milk is on fire. there is a cave of treasure, wrapped in yellow 'caution' tape, between your ribcage & spine. turning milk into fire is an effort. & now the milk is everywhere, it is turning into treasure in front of your spine. it is turning into fool's gold behind your ribcage. if the shoes are white & the tights are white & the sheet is white, then it is a ghost. made you look. & that is how milk is fake. just kidding. the milk is turning into plasma, it is looking like a ghost looking for treasure, looking like a jackpot. there is a map in the shoe. whose shoe? the ghost's shoe. the map says to get to the cave of treasure i must, first, drink a glass of milk fire, & then, climb into your ear without using my hands. by the time i get to your ribcage the television is a ghost & your spine smells like overcooked plasma. now i am looking like a ballerina. finally, i make it to the treasure cave. there is a button. i am exhausted. i push the button. a recording of your voice plays, you say, "sorry, i am unable to get to the treasure right now, leave your name & milk fire & i will call you back." i put a sheet over my head & tuck myself in for the night. you are warm.

richard brautigan

richard brautigan walks into a store & buys everything but us. we are on sale & reaching our expiration date but richard brautigan has good taste. at home, richard brautigan measures the surface area of all richard brautigan's regrets. the number is greater than the flavor of roasted beets & less than deceit. richard brautigan never pays for a massage. only once has richard brautigan stood on a bridge & yelled: i am a constipated vessel of wonderment. richard brautigan folds his socks into cotton cranes because he can, because he is richard brautigan & we are nothing but dented cans of food, pretending to be everything.

this is why people move to foreign countries full of bad weather

sometimes people die. so:

first, leave the sink running & travel to a country
you have never been to & will never leave. forget
the facts & amnesia everyone from yourself.

then, find the biggest city in this new country.
you will know this city by the smell of hard
boiled eggs.

it is best to sit in a park in the middle of the busy city,
just watching people. imagining. you can imagine the
people friends, family, lovers, acquaintances. it is easier
this way. this way, there is no pain &, so, death becomes
an abstraction because you won't know anyone. you
will
only know fictions of people that could be, the
passersby.
sometimes people die. when you love them
before they die, even if you don't think you do,
or don't remember that you do; you can't really tell
until after the person is dead. this is the point
of death & the reason love exists.

this morning a man is caught in a difficult place.
he is between the subway & the subway tracks.
it is rush hour, which makes this even more sad.
many of the people are angry at the man.
he might have jumped, he might have slipped or been

pushed. nobody in the subway station cares, they are just angry to be late for work. sometimes people die. he will, you hope not today. imagine the man is family & sit in the park. never go to work. sit there not doing anything, try to heal the man with imaginary pain. sometimes people die.

when she leaves for work the morning looks like a commotion. he gets out of bed & looks at the wall where a mirror should be. instead of a reflection, he is shadow. there is a razor & a mason jar & for a shadow, he is not famous. yesterday was between the toes. today will be the back of the neck. he lay himself on the kitchen table like he is made of gravity. she is an audience in another city. hanging off the table, his head is perpendicular to the mason jar. it will only be a small gash because art is important, but not valuable. the morning is misshapen & he is holding a razor. he budgets a small line across the back of his neck, an incomplete barcode. the mason jar collects each drop. once full, he seals the mason jar & stores it with the others. his refrigerator is a mausoleum of liquid ruby. he calls the work, "no use for blood, until you return." he never wanted to become an artist, but each day, she asks him to.

i'm sorry clouds

imagine the trauma that gave the sky the blues

past the sky's blues is the deep black

we're in outer space because it is not possible
to breathe in outer space
yet here we are and the idea
of our us is comfort
like the idea of the air
back on earth

thumbs up
to being the dish soap in your life
to cryogenically frozen prisms as occupation

without your you
a river of lava in a blizzard
is my emotional credit score

a lightning bolt on your tongue tip
sunglasses and a scythe

i'm on the brink of blood blister and blue
as you cover my body with sesame seeds
for the first time

she asked him about his life. he said it was like waiting in line to board an airplane, except the final destination was always the next connecting leg. she asked him if that was so bad. he said the time spent on airplanes was the real part of life & that the rest of the time we dreamt about flying & also having real lives, like the kind you can buy in the sky mall magazine.

she asked him if it was bad etiquette to paint one's toe nails on an airplane. he said it depended on how the nails looked naked & if the other passengers were provided with nose plugs, which sometimes happened, on real airplanes. she asked him if he thought she'd look pretty dressed as a casino. he said that did not sound so bad.

she asked him if he counted the cars from his window seat. he said it was easier to count lakes but that once he had tried to count snow, but the 'altitude' made him drink seltzer water from a small plastic cup, so, he ended up forgetting how many sides make a snow flake. she asked him if it was ok to do that. absolutely, he said, because, that's what he said.

she asked him what his favorite part of flying was. he said oh, breaking the silence of clouds, though, he enjoyed the way older airplanes still had ash trays that made him think about volcanology. she asked him if he wished he could sit on the wing when the airplane

was crowded. he said that the doors only opened from
the inside, so, no, he would get too lonely.

she asked him why the pilot was so important. he said
that from the front of the airplane, the pilot was closest
to the horizon & could see god's weather mistakes. she
asked him about his life. he said put on your oxygen
mask. she asked water. he said sure. she asked exit row.
he said cabin pressure. she asked more peanuts, please.
he said no smoking in the lavatory.

Let Me Be Your Tongue

will become

the morning your boots are filled with so much gravity that it is impossible to walk up or fall down a hill, will be the morning before violence. on this morning, the edge of the horizon will be at arm's length, yet you will not be able to make a fist. the wind will blow the ocean out of itself. piles of shimmering fish will form mountains of wet flesh. on top of these cold blooded mountains, pianos will play themselves to tears. every living cicada will hover above you, forming a circle, clicking their abdomen in and out. on the morning before violence, a bird will bend the pitch of its song into a ring of black light. the only secret left will be how to wear the clouds like clothes. all speculation will become a pattern of calm, and various bacterium will make love to themselves inside of your body.

sky of the floating oceans

the walk to the bridge
is more difficult than
the walk across

roads are our attempt
against chaos

we dig holes
to fill voids

we've been holding moon
light in our palms
fists clenched shut

we scream into envelopes
& mail ourselves
our own echoes

our dust is the physical
form of dream space

each step moves us
closer to the light
& also the darkness

on one side of the mountain
we know light
on the other side
all else

without gravity the oceans
will fall from the earth
& so will we

to be two embracing
fossils in an ocean
of dirt is enough

remember when we were gold

remember us beside the deadline?
you: the carbonation inside my gold
tooth. me saying: catch me
in the mouth you gift house.
remember when we were tangled
without the clothing
in constellation humor?

when we were like whales
with obsessive compulsive disorder
swimming in the largest circles
looking for each other in the deepest
parts of each other, becoming
the zero.

do you remember feeding me
spam in the bath & how we read
the sonogram bubbles on the back
of your arm?

when instead of getting an m.f.a.
we laid in the very center
of the kitchen floor &
syllabically whispered
czhech
o
slo
va
ki

a
into the very center
of each other for four
days.

remember when we were gold
like the last tooth
& how we shone
like a flashlight
in a whale's mouth?

i can only wish for my teeth
to fall out of my head
when the sky is the color
of your skin.

i can only wish to last
as long as glitter
on your achilles
heel.

remember how love
spelled backwards isn't
what we are
or a question.

popping gold

while the brain is in another room
i want pure success
the eye speaking to the soul

while the universe circles around itself
a fish cries in its sleep

infinity is defined by the relationship
between colors and emotions

everywhere the air is sick there is thirst in the neck
the sadness glows the sadness is glowing
the wind is becoming the crease in your elbow
& eventually the sun will fail itself

i conjure moon blood
when a fire starts to burn
because i've never known what to do
except cry gold

doors are much easier
when the walls of the room
don't exist

like when whale sharks
french kiss each other without an audience
like that

i've never seen a mirror i've liked

unless i've been crying
then i become real

i am constantly pouring wet concrete onto gravity
& lighting snow on fire at dawn
i don't want to lose my voice
i want it to burst into every gold molecule
stuck to your skin

every great city will eventually have a great fire. just as dying is the slow process of drying out, becoming a lemon peel. i'll be waiting for you at the edge of the great fire with my expensive teeth. just as the sorrow of blindness is alleviated by the smell of your shadow, or some shit like that. i have the same dream on different nights. while you sleep, i set our house on fire and then rescue you, wiping the soot from your brow, playing the hero with you in my arms. just do something guttural every time. be a night without moon. be the intrinsic color of water. be blue. just live like the movement of fire is calculated, like fire is the suspect & what we do inside of our insides is the crime. just as the sorrow of shadows is the smell of blindness, or some shit like that. eventually the great fire will fall from grace & we will become lemon peels a long way from home.

a large mouth that dissolves into light

blinking takes too much time
so i discard my eyelids
to better focus
on the inevitable
the great joy of being chased
by an enormous fish

i want to steal a mouth
throw each tooth
into the ocean & walk
until each grows back

i want to be the lyric
o to be a virus
with no worth
but in the consumption
of order

i want three wishes
first to be placed
under your foot
second to be crushed
by you
third to be your you

at the very least
give me infinite mouths
& call me diamond
at the very most

give me powers unknown
& turn me
into a large mouth
that dissolves
into light
there is no silence
in love
yet to the left
is the sun
& to the right
is the sun

as i look
in both directions
i do something
that takes away my breath
imagine everything
is not made of light
that organic matter
does not expire

how unlucky
to be human
but how lucky
to keep pace
with life

the cold is longer than the day

& it is amazing to see all of the circles
their perimeters touching the nothing the everything
& yet so round
the shape of the face of a ghost inside of a tear
i am nothing if not the flavor of a red wind
what if the sun & the light do not meet what then of
the day
& how your mind is longer than a row of deserts
is why & where i have loved you
standing in front of your you i cannot here you
the streets are calling themselves teeth black black
teeth miles of throat
the loudest sound is in the breaking of a
hummingbird's wing
like trying to repeat something that has yet to happen
imagine that which is not
i love you like i am not an animal of dirt
the dirt between my teeth misspells itself
the dirt is all that's left of this
to be a romantic dirt is why we persist
why we throw dirt into the air
until we become the entrance

& argue with the schedule of autumnal light

strange night

i would take you even part time in the pasture
in the eyes or congregating on the cheek
i want you   a profound thing pretending to happen
the pasture is a type of madness
where giant lanterns in your shape
keep the darkest of night warm
there is a sense of calm in the word pebble
the forest is on the verge of an emotional break down
i offer the forest support offer the forest everything
you are so much paper & light
how does it feel to be a lantern or at least a metaphor
the forest is full of mud the mud is full of danger
you are full of tiny apples
the moon is not synthetic it is a moon
i fill a pail with moonbeams and offer them
to the forest   the forest is full of tears
the pines are an elaborate opera about death
i will be ready to die once i stop feeling
the moon is alive & shaking the wind
the forest is shaking & sending its pines
to the edge of the pasture where darkness stands
& teaches night the meaning of precipice
i would take you even as endless knives

shadow of no doubt

but trees really do sleep and we grow
and crack until the light comes

if i could place anything in my eyes
i'd choose the moment before you
die so that you never would
so i'm placing that moment now

when i've trouble sleeping i think of anything
opaque i imagine what trees dream of
i cut our dreams in two and trade halves
with myself

let's stare into each other's pores and count
backward from infinity

                              last night
i cut a hole in my arm and planted
the seeds of a weeping willow
you are a talented sleeper

when a tree falls in a forest
we twist ourselves into something obscure

can i hold onto your you like a fist
full of steam until my ghost
dies and becomes a ghost
or at least your favorite
tree

types of things

when you pretended
to kiss me
on the exact
piece of skin
where my eyelids meet
my eye lashes
i wasn't thinking

about you or the time
it takes a finger
to hit a piano key
& the sound
to make your ears work

or how poorly house plants do
when you're always out
looking for that one thing
that is just like
all the other things

i wasn't thinking about whales
or pollution or being a child
or what it was like to be a child
or the way your words taste
when it has been raining
in the back of your mind

or about the way little things
make us hide

from littler things
like the sound of a mosquito
coughing

i wasn't thinking
about those types of things
or about what it would be like
to pretend to kiss you
on your exact
piece of skin
that you're pretending
is not the most beautiful
thing since all things
were named & grew
in pulchritude or any other
kind of beauty

living sculpture

i don't understand all of this but you are a palindrome from i. & because of this i am up in the middle of the sky with a pair of topiary shears, turning the clouds into inorganic shapes. i am in the sky taking out my eyes and gluing them to your shadow. i am in the sky, without eyes. i am in you like serious & stuffing the clouds with moss. i am throwing clouds everywhere. these are still clouds, but, yes, i have covered them with inorganic stained glass, ok? what else am i supposed to do, while you attract all of that light? it isn't that love is complicated, but that we are called human beings. it isn't that i am in the sky, but i am. i am in the middle of the sky as the stained glass light topples toward the earth and onto your shadow, the one to which my eyes are glued. i don't understand all of this but you are a palindrome for i.

you don't get better, worse, or stay the same. you are all of the above. you are greater than the sum & are all of the parts. the worst part of your you is me. creeley said: you are not me, nor i you. i wish i were both & you were a photograph of your you, something that can fly to where beginning and end meet. i am cheating on myself with you over & over until again. you are the place poets call precipice, where i go to explode. this world is imperfect for a lack of nouns naming you. the finding is the hardest part, but o i love that chair, the one in which you just sat.

Year of the Wet Heart

kindling

write your name on fire
and forget everything

these days
it's impossible
not to be jealous
of a prism

for the safety of those
around you please return
to an elemental state

levitate
your hesitations
spray paint
your third eye
embrace loosely
connected notations

this is the 21st
century you are almost
made of neon
light

all of the blood
in your body
is extra
celestial making
you: infinity

light everything
on fire and forget
your name   here

resolutions

beginning is the intersection
of nothing left &
waking as a mode
of abstraction

what gravity would do
to my anxieties
is akin to lava
meeting an ice shelf

the sonic texture of interruption

i am beautiful
throwing lasagna at the television

every day is the beginning
of a new year spent
trying to become invisible
without dying

the body as vapor
acid trail visual as manifesto
opening up the sky
is the goal

the last piano in a desert
blizzard isn't enough

the turbulence is oceanic

it's called having a brain

unfortunately
death is telepathic

when your face begins

leaking   slap the wind

in its face. you have hands

& the wind can't cry.

if you don't laugh

when you fall out

of a tree   you aren't climbing

high enough. this is your only

chance to break something

in your body. wow

you can break it

& it can heal itself.

this is proof that existence

exists. somewhere in the city

a thing eats a smaller thing.

love everything even if it rips

you in half

so many times

what floats

there is absence

in my mouth.

darkness can't exist

under this tongue.

even the idea

of nothing has

been expelled from

my field of

gums. & where

have you been?

out in the

world searching for

the origin of

guilt: a substance

that adheres human

dreams to themselves.

i love you

even after nothing.

i thank the skin

under your feet

each morning.

feet are tough

in that they are

like grandmothers

who haven't sold

all their tears

to the city.

our blood type is

tragedy & hair

is only here to fall

off us & on

to the street.

sadness is hair

floating through air

looking for any

body.

hold it in until you burst

if diamonds travel through the blood

stream swallow the moon immediately

compare the lungs of a whale

to the size of your psychic debt

the respectful thing to do is make

the disappointing choice like the human

meat you've always been

o beatific lump of confusion

sadness is still blue even in the black

emptiness of space   in the tight room of death

floating above the initial hurt

we are never overlooked by mistakes

nor the color of boredom

by accepting the weight of limitation

you've lost the ability to be tree to be light

the quality of the universe is mediocre

and i am the wrong thought every time

shadow/light

the greatest kindness
is the acceptance of perpetual loss

sorrow perches behind the mirage
of a million smiling lips

what a time for a stomach
stuffed with stones & coconut husk

tears are meant for sitting
at a desk beside a drawer
opening itself to be filled by any
piece of junk mail

o toes
only attached to us
to feel the farthest reaches
of human sorrow

tomorrow an egg will crack
open & sun beams will splash
light on a bird yet to consider
death

find a living thing
to wrap in a blanket
posthaste

if luck is in the room
write a resplendent elegy
for the destruction caused
by the opposable thumb

what a time
to be a late afternoon
kitchen window prism

surprise, surprise

of course i'm throwing paper airplanes
past the edge of death with you
i'm looking at you and every sentence
begins   *poetry is…*

i'm made out of a brain in great collapse
i'm falling over the edge of sky into your you

what did you eat for dinner
how many times do you breathe
before getting out of bed   these are my
essential oils

i'm sure of it now   you are
all of the things the wind can carry
and also the thing that carries the wind

of course i'm following you onto the airplane
made entirely of birds with metal wings
the safest place to be is in the air

we each wear gold rings and are therefore more
aerodynamic
i could start making sense   without ever letting
you know
but surprise surprise i wouldn't do that
before winter with its gloves for catching
anything but a body

underwater mirror

as you aren't thirsty
until you've seen the ocean

                the sky remains

                beautiful

                whether you do

                or do not

wandering the hall

of the truncated spirit
is the name
attached to my emotional labor

the realization that
crying is the act
of taking the negative
out of yourself
& that it can
also be called
shattered glass

i am learning
how to feel
tropical
on the inside

the milky way as fog on night
meaning
we will survive
even if we must die
to do it

evade all who kill
your vibes
in other words
jump off
the world immediately

don't worry
champagne is served in space

if you can't climb
a tree every day
at least imagine
yourself doing so
this speaks
to survival

exercise your futility
by arm wrestling
time
you both deserve a laugh

& as you fall
asleep
consider which
is the metaphor
    death
or
    death

take away my brain

the faucets are spewing
real life lava
& the vacuum with no off
switch has put a down
on a piece
of
my brain

even the forest is a city
if you squint
you'll miss the millennial
apocalypse

holographic ashes
in the wind i am goodbye
i am good by the river
where the wind plays
tree
i am good

buy a snake
to test friendships
this is the end
as it's always been
soon oxygen will be commoditized
& we will run from the sun
once worshipped

anything worth its weight

in regret will vibrate
through your hollow parts
searching for
the truth is an act of treason
against the natural
world

disagreeing with orange
is the new fatal flaw
o throw me
into the air
like gold
dipped
hot
dogs

species of crisis

who are we but a bridge built for a river
to cross over another river

at night we are the shape
of a   & at daybreak too

we contain 50% more hesitation
than the next leading mammal
yet we are never the quartz
nor the smoke

on our best days we are empty
on our worst: vibrant and human
still we are the thin line
between flying and falling

between learning and yearning
we are the thin line made to curve
forced to circle
around what we can't see
but know is there

we are the instinct before the warning

during the crossover   the last transition
we are the rain in tokyo
& the humidity   we: extra layer of clothing

we are the flowers of uncertainty

defying the wind

we are what is left
after space & time
uncouple

water drop

6/23/18, Haʻikū, Maui. Written in the palm garden of W.S. Merwin.

without me the clouds would assume
a different shape
& the ocean would weigh less
i am generous
allowing ants to walk through me
letting them become momentary
paperweights you do not need
to thank me for the fire
in the blossom of the ginger
nor the mud you sink

                    into

as you grow closer to the center
of the earth that contains us
my favorite place is in the throat
of the thrush
the lubricant for song infinitum
through me you see all the colors
that've been & will be
i assume nothing yet hold the cycle
of time within my shape
& if i am so lucky as to fall
onto your head
i will finally see the horizon
an illusion between sea & sky

vesper for the middle of the ocean

& already the rivers
run in reverse

& the least we can do
is help each other
put sky into our bodies

& even the protea have mothers
they can't remember

& from what i can't recall
death is without pants

& laughing again

& again we gather
to put something in
the ground that won't grow

& the goal has always been
to travel by echo in echo
an echo

& every place is particular
-ly pleasant without people

& even without gills
we all return
to water

& even without water
we all return
we all
        we

Acknowledgments

Thanks to the editors of the following magazines (some of which are now defunct) in which some of these poems have appeared in earlier forms: *Bluestem, Conveyor, Corium, decomP, elimae, Everyday Genius, Fleeting, Gesture, Heartcloud, Heavy Feather Review, Hobart, Housefire, Ilk, Imminent Quarterly, Indigest, iO, Juked, >kill author, leveler, The Merwin Conservancy, Mud Luscious, NAP, Otis Nebula, Pangur Ban Party, PANK, Powder Keg, Red Lightbulbs, Radar Poetry, Requited, Shabby Doll House, Smalldoggies, Spork, Thrush, The Underwater Railroad Used Furniture Review, Vinyl, Word Riot,* **and** *wtf pwm*

I also send my deepest aloha to the following people, who have all played a role in the development of my brain, my spirit, and my poetic relationship to the universe: Camille Dungy, Truong Tran, Matthew Clark Davison, Mike Skott McCullough, Britt Melewski, Charlie Getter, Nic Alea, Evan Karp, Carrie Lorig, Matt L. Roar, Molly Prentiss, The Williamsburg Crunchers, J. Brandon Loberg, Jonathan Siegel, Ariana Reines, Naomi Shihab-Nye, my family, and Tess Patalano.